Drs. Les & Leslie
Parrott

AUTHORS OF
THE COMPLETE GUIDE TO MARRIAGE MENTORING

A
TEN-SESSION
PROGRAM FOR
EQUIPPING
MARRIAGE
MENTORS

MARRIAGE MENTOR
TRAINING MANUAL
for HUSBANDS

ZONDERVAN™

GRAND RAPIDS, MICHIGAN 49530 USA

ZONDERVAN.COM/
AUTHOR**TRACKER**

ZONDERVAN™

Marriage Mentor Training Manual for Husbands
Copyright © 2006 by The Foundation for Healthy Relationships

Requests for information should be addressed to:

Zondervan, *Grand Rapids, Michigan 49530*

ISBN-10: 0-310-27165-7
ISBN-13: 978-0-310-27165-9

All Scripture quotations, unless otherwise indicated, are taken from the *Holy Bible: New International Version*®. NIV®. Copyright © 1973, 1978, 1984 by International Bible Society. Used by permission of Zondervan. All rights reserved.

The website addresses recommended throughout this book are offered as a resource to you. These websites are not intended in any way to be or imply an endorsement on the part of Zondervan, nor do we vouch for their content for the life of this book.

Published in association with Yates & Yates, LLP, Attorneys and Counselors, Suite 1000, Literary Agent, Orange, CA.

Interior design by Beth Shagene

Printed in the United States of America

07 08 09 10 11 12 • 21 20 19 18 17 16 15 14 13 12 11 10 9 8 7 6 5 4 3 2

Marriage Mentor Training Manual

for HUSBANDS

Resources by Les and Leslie Parrott

Books
51 Creative Ideas for Marriage Mentors
Becoming Soul Mates
The Complete Guide to Marriage Mentoring
Getting Ready for the Wedding
I Love You More (and workbooks)
Just the Two of Us
Love Is
The Love List
Love Talk (and workbooks)
The Marriage Mentor Training Manual for Husbands (for Wives)
Meditations on Proverbs for Couples
Pillow Talk
Questions Couples Ask
Relationships (and workbook)
Saving Your Marriage Before It Starts (and workbooks)
Saving Your Second Marriage Before It Starts (and workbooks)

Video Curriculum — ZondervanGroupware™
Complete Resource Kit for Marriage Mentoring
I Love You More
Love Talk
Mentoring Engaged and Newlywed Couples
Relationships
Saving Your Marriage Before It Starts

Audio Pages®
Love Talk
Relationships
Saving Your Marriage Before It Starts
Saving Your Second Marriage Before It Starts

Books by Les Parrott
The Control Freak
Helping Your Struggling Teenager
High Maintenance Relationships
The Life You Want Your Kids to Live
Seven Secrets of a Healthy Dating Relationship
Shoulda, Coulda, Woulda
Once Upon a Family
25 Ways to Win with People (coauthored with John Maxwell)
Love the Life You Live (coauthored with Neil Clark Warren)

Books by Leslie Parrott
If You Ever Needed Friends, It's Now
God Loves You Nose to Toes (children's book)
Marshmallow Clouds

CONTENTS

THE GIANT AWAKENS

In our book *The Complete Guide to Marriage Mentoring* we devote an introductory chapter to "the sleeping giant in the church." That's what we have called marriage mentoring for more than a decade. Why? Because, for too long, an invaluable and gigantic resource—namely, you and countless couples like you—has lain dormant, untapped. But that's beginning to change. The very fact that you are reading these words is proof of that.

You are among what we pray will be an increasingly powerful band of marriage mentors responsible for inciting the single, greatest social revolution of our day—the dramatic reduction of divorce in our lifetime. Think of the couples and children who will be impacted by our efforts!

We know you share this dream of ours: making marriages better. So right at the start of your training, before you even begin to roll up your sleeves, allow us to encourage you by something we wrote in *The Complete Guide to Marriage Mentoring*:

> There are close to 400,000 churches in America. If just one-third of these churches would recruit and train ten mentor couples each, that would mean one million marriage mentors. Think of the difference that would make!

You are creating that difference. Your decision to volunteer, to train, and to serve other couples as marriage mentors will make all the difference in the world. Do you believe it? Surely we can save half of the 1.2 million marriages that end in divorce each year if we continue to awaken the slumbering giant of marriage mentoring. And think of the marriages that can move from good to great if only another couple with more experience was willing to walk alongside.

Well, we won't have to imagine much longer. As we crisscross this country conducting marriage seminars in a wide variety of churches, we have met enough couples, just like you, to know that something big is about to happen. We are encouraged. The giant is indeed waking up. And the training program you hold in your hand is expressly designed to make sure "the giant" wakes up *with a purpose.*

In the pages of this training manual we promise to give you all the tools we know to give for becoming effective marriage mentors. We don't pretend that this program will fully equip you for every minute issue you might ever encounter with a mentoree couple, but it *will* prepare you to approach this task with confidence. And we promise to continue to resource you through additional helps as well as through our website, www.RealRelationships.com.

We thought of you frequently as we developed every aspect of this manual. We've prayed for you too. We've asked God to give you wisdom as you give that same wisdom to the couples you mentor. And we know he will.

Les and Leslie Parrott

THE PRELIMINARIES

SHOULD WE DO THIS TRAINING IN A GROUP OR ON OUR OWN?

Because we want to eliminate any hurdles that may exist in getting a marriage mentoring ministry off the ground, we have designed our training program to be flexible—so that it can be implemented in a small church of just a few dozen to a megachurch with thousands, by individual couples in the comfort of their own home or in a group of any size. This session of the manual will elaborate on how the training can be used best in either an individual couple or group setting.

If you are doing the training as an individual couple, proceed to the section titled "How Marriage Mentors Learn Best" on the next page. If you are doing the training in a group setting, we suggest that you spend ten to fifteen minutes introducing yourselves to the rest of the couples and, depending on the time available, answering at least one of the following questions:

- How did the two of you meet?
- How did you get engaged? Describe the proposal.
- Why are you interested in marriage mentoring?

How Marriage Mentors Learn Best

We have taught university courses for nearly two decades. And because our university takes teaching seriously, we often are required to attend workshops on "pedagogy" (pronounced *ped-a-go-gee*), a five-dollar word meaning "methods of instruction." As professors, we want to know how our students best learn a particular subject, so we in turn can use techniques and tools to help them internalize it and be able to use their new knowledge effectively.

We've given that same serious attention to exploring how you, as marriage mentors, will absorb, retain, and practice the information you'll be learning in this program. We conducted research on mentors-in-training. We've done pre- and post-tests to know what works and what doesn't. We've even conducted research with control groups to know if a particular piece of training makes any difference.

We say all this to let you know that this program is designed with great intention. And as you will soon see, it relies heavily on interaction. Sure, you will read a bit of content, complete a few self-tests, and view some real-live mentors on the training DVD. But much of your learning will take place as you talk with each other—husband and wife. Indeed, you'll learn more from what you say to each other than you will from any lecture, workshop, or seminar on this subject.

Why Do We Need Two Training Manuals?

You may be thinking, *This is a couple's training program. Can't we just share a manual?* It's a fair question. But let us tell you why having two manuals—his and hers—is essential for this training.

First, you will see that each manual has a session specific to that manual. This is where we speak directly to husbands and directly to wives about what they uniquely bring to the table of marriage mentoring. Each of us is hardwired differently for this task, and to be effective we need to give serious attention to our gender differences as marriage mentors—so that we might use them to our advantage with our mentorees.

Second, even if these unique sections were not included, it's important to complete many of the exercises on your own—before you explore them with your spouse. If you were to see your spouse's answers to particular questions before you answer the same questions yourself, it would influence your response and drain energy and authenticity from your training sessions.

Allow us to illustrate our point by having you do a brief exercise right now.

NOTE: Before beginning the exercise, become familiar with our simple system of symbols for types of exercises throughout the manual:

☕ = An exercise to complete on your own

☕ ☕ = An exercise to complete with your spouse,
typically a discussion of an on-your-own exercise

☕ ☕ ☕ = An exercise to complete couple to couple
or in a larger group

Exploring Potential Fears of Marriage Mentoring (5 MINUTES)

☕ Complete the following two sentence-stems as best as you can — without consulting your wife to do so.

In beginning this training program on marriage mentoring, my greatest fear is . . .

In beginning this training program on marriage mentoring, my wife's greatest fear is . . .

☕ ☕ Once you both have taken a minute to complete these sentences, compare notes. Are the answers your wife gave ones you would have predicted? Do you now know something new about each other that you didn't know just five minutes ago?

You get the point. This workbook will have dozens of opportunities for the two of you to talk with each other; and to make these conversations all they can be, you'll each need your own gender-specific training manual.

Of course, beyond two separate manuals from which to work, there are other ways to ensure you get as much out of this training as possible. We offer suggestions for doing just that in the next section.

How to Get the Most from This Book and Accompanying DVD

George, age ninety-two, and Jane, age eighty-nine, are all excited about their decision to get married. While out for a stroll to discuss wedding plans, they happen to pass a drugstore and stop in. George asks to speak to the owner.

"We're about to get married," George informs him. "Do you sell heart medication?"

"Of course we do," the owner replies.

"How about support hose to help with poor circulation?"

"Definitely."

"What about medicine for rheumatism, osteoporosis, and arthritis?" George continues.

"All kinds," says the owner with confidence.

"How about waterproof furniture covers and Depends?"

"Yessir."

"Hearing aids, denture supplies, and reading glasses?" the groom-to-be asks.

"Yes."

"What about eyedrops, sleeping pills, Geritol, and Ensure?"

"Absolutely."

"Do you sell wheelchairs, walkers, and canes?"

"All kinds and sizes," the owner replies. "But why all these questions?"

George smiles and proudly announces, "We'd like to use your store as our bridal registry."

Who can blame them? They're simply preparing, in very practical terms, for their journey together. And that's what we want to do next: prepare you for where you're going as a marriage mentor couple, equipping you with what you'll need to make this training experience the best it can be.

We'll begin with a quick overview of where we're headed, then a look at what's required of you, followed by some simple suggestions for maximizing your experience, and a final note on how to use each of the marriage mentoring resources available to you.

Where We're Headed

Before beginning a new journey, it's always helpful to chart the course. So let's survey the territory ahead.

Here, in session 1, we are merely giving you a few suggestions on how to use these marriage mentoring resources effectively.

In session 2, we paint a big picture of marriage mentoring. In other words, we make sure you understand "the concept" and how it works.

In session 3, we roll up our proverbial sleeves and take a good look at how your gender — as a man — impacts the marriage mentoring process. You see, what you bring to this process, by virtue of your biology, is different from what your wife brings to it.

In sessions 4 – 9, we teach you the time-tested skills you'll need as you work with your mentorees. These skills are universal, applicable to any and every age and stage of marriage, whether you are mentoring newlyweds or couples in distress.

Finally, in session 10, we help you hone your personal marriage mentoring style by having you explore the three "mentor tracks" to see which one you most lean toward. We also discuss the tremendous benefits of augmenting your marriage mentoring efforts with a small-group experience that your mentorees can plug into.

How It Works

We hope you have already read *The Complete Guide to Marriage Mentoring*. But if you haven't, you can read it along the way. Think of that book as your "textbook" to accompany this training manual. You'll get far more out of this program if you read *The Complete Guide* — and it will serve as a good reference long after your training is complete.

Typically your ten training sessions will be about fifty to sixty minutes in length and here's how the topics break down:

Session	Topic	DVD
1	Introduction	none
2	The Big Picture: An Overview of Marriage Mentoring	8 min.
3	Marriage Mentoring as a Man	3 min.
4	Building Rapport/Walking in Another Couple's Shoes	12 min.
5	Working as a Team/Agreeing on Outcomes	12 min.
6	Asking Meaningful Questions/Listening Aggressively	12 min.
7	Fielding Questions/Telling Your Stories	12 min.
8	Praying Together/Staying Sharp	12 min.
9	Being Yourself and Going with the Flow	8 min.
10	The Next Steps	10 min. (incl. 6 min. of promos)

As you can see, most of the sessions will include a DVD component to better illustrate the lesson. And each session will include opportunities for you to interact as a couple.

What's Required of You

If you're like most busy couples, you don't want your time to be wasted. We understand. That's why this material has been trimmed of anything superfluous and organized so that you use the training time productively. Of course, it still requires time. If you are doing the training in a structured group session, that time has been determined for you. If you are doing it as an individual couple, you will need to impose your own structure; we'll help you do that later in this session.

For now, we want you to know that your training time commitment is relatively minimal — ten hours or less — though we provide options along the way where you can choose to add further study.

In addition to some of your time, we also require all of your heart. Sounds a bit daunting, we know. But it's true. If you are going to be an effective marriage mentor, your heart needs to be in it. This is not something you can dabble in to see how you feel about it. Your mentorees have a built-in radar detector for phoniness and they'll see right through you.

Let's do a brief checkup to evaluate your current circumstances and motivation.

Exploring Personal Hurdles and Motivation (5 MINUTES)

List the top three things that are pulling for your time and energy right now. These may be things on the home front, with friends, or at work.

_____

_____

_____

Now rate how motivated you are right now to become trained as a marriage mentor. Be honest. You don't have to be at a perfect 10 to continue. You just need to be up front.

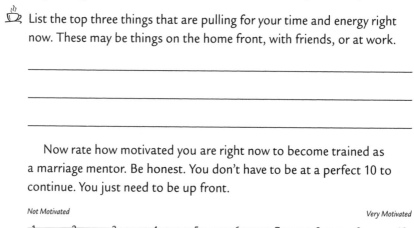

Not Motivated   Very Motivated

1   2   3   4   5   6   7   8   9   10

Once both you and your spouse have answered these questions in your separate training manuals, take a moment to debrief. Talk about the issues in your life that are pulling for your time. What can you do to help each other make the time you'll need to complete this training?

Also talk about your motivation level. If one of you is more motivated than the other, why is that? If either of you ranked your motivation level at less than 7, do you view this as temporary or are you convinced that marriage mentoring is not something you should commit to at this time? If so, it's best to postpone your training.

A Simple Suggestion

As with any new skill you want to learn or any new knowledge you want to absorb, you will get the most from this marriage mentor training program if you set aside potential distractions, anything that might interfere with the learning process. If you're a multitasker, this might be a challenge — especially if you're doing the training at home — because it means no email, cell phone, BlackBerry, radio, television, whatever.

We can almost feel some of you cringing. Okay, we're not policing you. But you know that you will only get out of this experience what you put into it. So we're simply urging you to give this training the attention it deserves.

Besides, you'll soon realize it's a lot of fun, and you're going to enjoy the benefit of the "boomerang effect" that you've read about (or will soon) in *The Complete Guide to Marriage Mentoring*.

NOTE: If you're doing this training as an individual couple, skip ahead to page 18 and the section titled "Marriage Mentor Training as an Individual Couple."

MARRIAGE MENTOR TRAINING IN A GROUP SETTING

If you are a part of a larger church or community that is launching or has already begun a marriage mentoring ministry, we recommend conducting your training in a group setting. Why? Because there is synergy in meeting together. You'll have common questions and concerns that a facilitator can address to all of you at once.

Most likely, your training facilitator will be a minister or a marriage mentor lead couple. Whether or not they have already completed the training themselves, they simply serve to structure the time, make sure the DVD equipment is ready to use, cover the logistics, and so on.

Choosing Your Schedule

There are three primary schedules for conducting group training. One is not better than the others. They are simply offered as a means to make this training fit your calendar and style.

- *Option 1: Eight to Ten Weekly Sessions.* This is a straightforward series of weekly sessions of about fifty to sixty minutes each, as illustrated in the table on page 15. Of course, even in this scenario you are free to condense the first two sessions and the last two sessions to make the series eight weeks instead of ten.
- *Option 2: Five Weekly Sessions.* In this scenario you would condense the training to five sessions of about ninety minutes each, covering two sessions each time you gather.
- *Option 3: A Weekend Training Retreat.* You may find it helpful to do all of the training in a single weekend gathering at your church or another getaway setting. On Friday evening you would cover the material from sessions 1 – 2 in about two and half hours of training (with time included for icebreaker activities). On Saturday you would cover the material from sessions 3 – 10 in another six hours of training.

Regardless of how you structure your training, we hope you will incorporate as much fun into it as you can. In a group setting you have the opportunity to interact not only as a couple but with other couples as well.

NOTE: If you are doing group training, you have now finished session 1 and are ready to consider the big picture of marriage mentoring. Please turn to page 21.

MARRIAGE MENTOR TRAINING AS AN INDIVIDUAL COUPLE

Some years ago a *Leadership Journal* cartoon depicted a layman talking with the pastor of his small church and included this caption: "Pastor Marv, we can't revive our church by implementing small groups—we are a small group!"

If you can identify with this cartoon you probably have already realized that your marriage mentoring ministry won't occur on a large scale. In fact, the marriage mentoring "team" in your local church may consist of only you and your wife. Not a problem. In fact, it speaks volumes about you and your passion to build better marriages in your community. You'll soon see that this program will work just fine in your setting.

Or maybe you are part of a larger church that has an ongoing marriage mentoring ministry and you are simply joining the program at a later point. There could be numerous reasons, besides being in a small church community, that you need to go through the training as an individual couple.

We want to assure you that your training as a marriage mentor couple will be every bit as successful as it would be if you were doing it in a group with other like-minded couples.

Setting Your Own Pace

Since your training is not determined by a larger schedule or program, you are free to proceed at your own pace. Take as much time as you like on any particular session. Complete one training session per week or do them all in a single weekend. That's up to you.

The only "must" is that the training needs to be done in tandem with your spouse. In other words, you will need to interact throughout your training. And while you can do a bit of reading and complete a few of the exercises on your own (without your partner present), you will eventually need to come together to process the material.

To help you set some structural guidelines at the outset, complete the following exercise:

What's Your Personal Approach to This Training? (5-10 MINUTES)

Select the item that best represents how you would complete these sentences:

I would rather . . .

☐ Go slowly without feeling pressured to complete the training by a certain date.

☐ Go quickly to get it done and get on with the practice of mentoring couples.

☐ Go at moderate rate with a scheduled pace and a specific completion date in mind.

I would rather . . .

☐ Complete multiple training sessions in a row for as long as we feel like it.

☐ Complete one of the ten training sessions each week to have the whole program completed ten weeks from now.

☐ Complete the training program in a weekend by having our own little mini marriage mentoring retreat.

I feel . . .

☐ Strongly about how we approach and schedule this training and I'm certain my way is best.

☐ Confident that my way will work but I'm open to how my spouse would like to approach this training as well.

☐ Very laid back about how we decide as a couple to do this training—I'm flexible and can go with whatever my spouse might like to do.

Now take a moment to compare your answers with your spouse's and determine together how you will go about your personal training. If need be, get out your calendar(s) and reserve the times that you will dedicate to this training.

What You Will Need for Your Sessions

Here's a checklist of items you will need for your training sessions:

- *The Complete Guide to Marriage Mentoring*
- *Marriage Mentor Training Manual for Husbands*
- *Marriage Mentor Training Manual for Wives*
- *Marriage Mentor Training and Recruiting* DVD
- A DVD player and television
- A pen or pencil for each of you
- A comfortable space for interacting with each other (free from distractions)
- Typically fifty to sixty minutes of uninterrupted time for each session, although sessions 9 and 10 are planned for only forty minutes (You may choose to spend more time in any given session if you desire.)

That's it. We've covered the preliminaries. You have the essentials in hand and you're ready to begin. In the next session we will take a look at the big picture of marriage mentoring.

THE BIG PICTURE

Corresponds to chapters 1 – 7
of *The Complete Guide to Marriage Mentoring.*

OVERVIEW OF THE MARRIAGE MENTOR TRIAD

In a few minutes you will watch a DVD presentation that features real-life couples, just like you, who are making a difference in the lives of other couples through marriage mentoring.

Before you view the DVD, however, let's consider two things: (1) how you would describe marriage mentoring, and (2) how your past relationships have prepared you for this experience. Please complete the following exercises now.

Defining Marriage Mentoring (5 MINUTES)

 Pretend you're Noah Webster for a moment and write your own "dictionary definition" of marriage mentoring in the space below. Don't discuss your definition with your spouse just yet. And don't get uptight about this. Our purpose is just to get you thinking. (When you watch the DVD, you'll see a definition of marriage mentoring which you can compare with the one you wrote here.)

Marriage mentoring (mer-ij men-təring):

Next, briefly jot down three or four personal qualities that you think will benefit you as a marriage mentor.

EXPERIENCE	LAngl @ ourselves
COmmiTmenT	FAiTh

 Now share your definition and mentoring qualities with your spouse and compare notes.

Our "Marriage Mentors" (10 MINUTES)

 Whether you have thought about them as "marriage mentors" or not, every married couple has other couples, or individuals, who have shaped or influenced their marriage in significant ways. These people may be your parents, relatives, friends, ministers, counselors, teachers, colleagues, or even people you have only read about but never met.

Take a few moments on your own to brainstorm names, and then put your heads together as a couple to actually build the list. Next to their name(s), write a single phrase or two that captures how they have positively influenced your marriage:

Name	How They "Mentored" Us
DAD	Life Long insTiTuTion

_____   _____

_____   _____

_____   _____

 If you are doing your training in a group setting, share one person or couple on your list and how they shaped your marriage. What can you learn about marriage mentoring from the informal mentoring relationships you and other couples have enjoyed? What did these people do for you, in specific terms, that you'd like to do for others?

 Play the DVD segment for session 2. (8 MINUTES)
Use the following space to take notes if you wish.

After viewing the DVD, what strikes you most about what you just saw? Briefly discuss this with your spouse and/or the group.

Now focus your thoughts on the marriage mentoring triad. As you just saw on the DVD, it is based on the idea that there are three main emphases or "tracks" that naturally occur in most marriage mentoring ministries:

1. *Preparing* engaged and newlywed couples
2. *Maximizing* good marriages to become great marriages
3. *Repairing* marriages in distress

This idea can be represented visually in the following diagram:

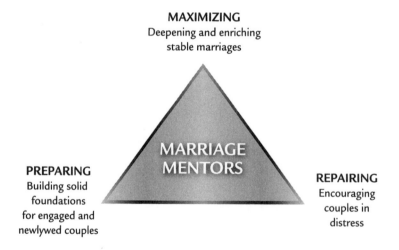

MAXIMIZING
Deepening and enriching
stable marriages

MARRIAGE
MENTORS

PREPARING
Building solid
foundations
for engaged and
newlywed couples

REPAIRING
Encouraging
couples in
distress

Do you, as a couple, feel inclined to work with couples in one of these tracks more than the others? Let's find out.

Which Track Do You Lean Into? (5 MINUTES)

At this juncture, we're not asking you to select a track that you'll stick with exclusively. After all, as you go through additional training sessions you are bound to learn more about your own marriage and where you are most gifted to mentor. But to help you begin thinking about what that "best fit" might be, place a number in each corner of the triangle below to represent your personal percentage of interest in mentoring the three categories of couples (added together, the three numbers should total 100):

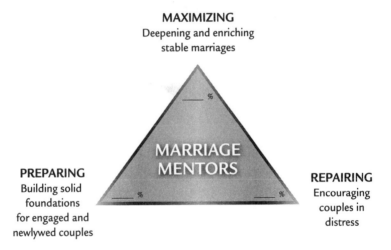

MAXIMIZING
Deepening and enriching
stable marriages

_____ %

MARRIAGE MENTORS

PREPARING
Building solid
foundations
for engaged and
newlywed couples

_____ %

REPAIRING
Encouraging
couples in
distress

_____ %

Again, compare your answers with your spouse's. How do your percentages line up? Do you both lean most naturally toward one group over the others? Briefly discuss why you answered the way you did. (Later in our training we will ask you to revisit this exercise.)

You've heard us talk about the "boomerang effect" of marriage mentoring—how, on occasion, you may get more out of these experiences than your mentorees. While this should never be your primary motive for mentoring other couples, it is still worth considering mentoring's "fringe benefits."

Exploring Our Potential "Boomerang Effect" (5 MINUTES)

The list of potential benefits of being a marriage mentor are unique to each couple. Following are a half dozen of the most common benefits we hear from other marriage mentors. Review the list, placing a check next to any and all that you think might apply to you. And note any that might not be on this list as well.

- ☐ Rekindle our romantic feelings
- ☐ Give us a shared mission
- ☐ Relive early memories we treasure
- ☐ Renew our appreciation of each other's abilities
- ☐ Create more lively conversations between us
- ☐ Help us learn more about ourselves

☐ Other: _____

☐ Other: _____

Share your list with your partner and discuss why you think a particular benefit will be important or valuable to you.

THE STRUCTURE OF A TYPICAL MARRIAGE MENTORING MINISTRY

Before ending this training session we want to highlight one other subject mentioned in the DVD segment: how a marriage mentoring ministry is structured. Our reason for reviewing it here in the manual is that we believe you will be a better mentor couple if you have a concept of where you fit into a mentoring program and how your gifts might be used best.

On the next page is a more detailed version of the diagram you saw depicted on the DVD. We provide it here for your reference. You'll also find this same diagram on page 220 of *The Complete Guide to Marriage Mentoring* as well as in a downloadable format at www.RealRelationships.com.

Structuring a Marriage Mentoring Ministry

How to Implement the Marriage Mentoring Triad

Pastor

Pastor Recruitment
1. Present the marriage mentoring team model
2. Pastor to recruit marriage mentor lead couple
3. Marriage mentor lead couple to recruit
   three marriage mentor track leaders

Marriage Mentor Lead Couple

Marriage Mentor Lead Couple Responsibilities
1. Spiritual leadership of the marriage triad
2. Recruitment, training, and equipping of marriage mentors
3. Point of contact for funneling couples into triad categories
4. Hosting small group leader training
5. Coordinating marriage enrichment events (retreats, etc.)
6. Certified trainer of assessment tools

Marriage Mentor Track Leaders

"Preparing   "Maximizing   "Repairing
Track"   Track"   Track"

Marriage Mentor Track Leaders Responsibilities
1. Provide supervision of their respective triad track
2. Become certified in their triad track
3. Point of contact for couples seeking track training
4. Recruit small group leaders for track
5. Certified trainer of track assessment tools
6. Promote track throughout the church

Small Group Couple Responsibilities
1. Take part in small group leadership track training
2. Take the respective track assessment and expanded diagnostic
3. Recruit small group participants for their small group
4. Promote track throughout the church
5. Commit to replicate their group every 18 months
   (raising up a small group leader couple from their group)

Small Group Leaders

"Preparing Track"   "Maximizing Track"   "Repairing Track"
Small Group Leaders   Small Group Leaders   Small Group Leaders

An Optional Assignment:
The Bible and Mentoring

Interested in exploring some of the biblical foundations of mentoring? Either now or before the next session you may find it helpful to have the following Bible study with your spouse.

> NOTE: If you are doing this training in a group setting and can extend your session beyond fifty minutes, you might consider pairing up two or three couples to explore these passages together.

Mentoring Relationships in Scripture

 If you have read *The Complete Guide to Marriage Mentoring*, you already know that the Bible is filled with many examples of mentoring. Here is a list of mentoring relationships from Scripture. Select any that you might like to read about.

- Eli and Samuel (1 Samuel 1 – 3)
- Elijah and Elisha (1 Kings 19:19 – 21)
- Moses and Joshua (Deuteronomy 31; Joshua 1)
- Naomi and Ruth (Ruth 1)
- Elizabeth and Mary (Luke 1:39 – 56)
- Barnabas and Paul (Acts 13 – 15)
- Paul and Timothy (Acts 16:1 – 5; 1 Timothy 4; 6:11 – 12)

After reading about each mentoring relationship that you chose, discuss what qualities made it successful.

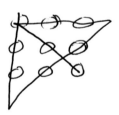

MARRIAGE MENTORING AS A MAN

MAN TO MAN:
HOW YOUR GENDER IMPACTS YOUR MENTORING

This session of your training manual is distinctly different from your wife's. In fact, we've prepared a DVD segment explaining why this session is so important and how the two of you can get the most from it.

But before you play the DVD segment, here's an exercise to help you consider how your gender differences will make you better marriage mentors.

The Differences Between Men and Women (8 MINUTES)

 What are the fundamental differences between men and women? List three or four as best you can.

Men   *Women*

_____   _____

_____   _____

_____   _____

_____   _____

Now compare your list of gender distinctions with your spouse's list. How are they similar? How are they different?

Play the DVD segment for session 3. (3 MINUTES)
Use the following space to take notes if you wish.

A PERSONAL MESSAGE FROM LES

Let's clear this up right from the top: You don't have to be the world's greatest husband to be an effective marriage mentor. Chances are this erroneous thought was one that kept you from more seriously contemplating mentoring before now. I can't tell you how many men have confided in me that their wives would like them to consider marriage mentoring, but they felt inadequate as husbands. If that's where you're coming from, I want to allay your fears immediately. In fact, complete the following exercise to highlight my point.

The Perfect Husband (4 MINUTES)

This exercise is just for you. You won't need to explore it with your wife or anyone else. Simply list up to six qualities that, in your mind, describe the perfect husband.

_____	_____
_____	_____
_____	_____

Now, how many husbands do you know who are perfect? Of course, you don't know a single one. As you review the list you've just created, you may know some husbands who do these things better than you. That's okay. These are qualities to aspire to. By the way, you'll be amazed at how becoming a marriage mentor will help you become the husband you aspire to be.

With this simple fact made plain, let's turn our attention to what we as men bring to the marriage mentoring enterprise. It has to do with our hard-wiring. You see, as a general rule, we're about "analyzing" while women are about "sympathizing." And this distinction, if understood, can be a tremendous asset to marriage mentoring.

SPEAKING HER SYMPATHETIC LANGUAGE

I'll say it again: men analyze and women sympathize. Of course, there are women who are primarily analytical and men who are primarily sympathetic. Indeed, for about 10 percent of couples, the typical roles are reversed. And certainly, most people use both skills to varying degrees.

Nevertheless, relative to men, most women are focused on the here-and-now. While you are analyzing plans and solving problems for a better tomorrow, your wife is focused on what's going on right now between the two of you—or, in the case of marriage mentoring, the four of you.

Why does this matter? Because you can become significantly more effective as a mentoring husband if you are aware of this difference. Not only that, but you can become a more effective mentor as you learn to pay a little less attention to the "report" (just getting the facts from your mentorees in order to solve their problems) and a little more to your wife's sympathetic "rapport" (and how it impacts your present relationship with the process of marriage mentoring). Here's how:

First, rate how much you want—truly desire—to build rapport with your partner as well as your mentoree couple. How much do you really want to have conversations that bring you closer together? Be honest. Use this scale to make it concrete.

No Desire   Intense Desire

1   2   3   4   5   6   7   8   9   10

This simple rating is important because it forces you to own up to what may be your biggest obstacle in crossing the communication gender line. If you truly have very little desire to "connect" (if you ranked it 4 or lower), you probably have more going on than simple gender differences. You may feel wounded or deeply misunderstood, or perhaps even have a biological issue that requires medical help. On average, most men in a typical relationship rank the desire for rapport at about 7. We want to build rapport with our wife, but it isn't necessarily our highest felt need. And it is often even lower when connecting with others, such as mentorees.

Does this mean we'll never be effective as marriage mentors? Hardly. In fact, we have something tremendously valuable to bring to the process. Our analytical inclinations are important. They tend to keep marriage mentoring on task and headed to a desirable outcome.

Once you have reflected on your desire to use and appreciate what is likely your wife's sympathetic leanings in a marriage mentoring meeting, take a few of minutes to explore this with her.

How will different gender hardwiring impact your marriage mentoring?

How can you use each other's gender strengths to be a better marriage mentoring team? Be specific.

WHEN IT'S TIME TO MENTOR MAN TO MAN

One question we are often asked by mentors-in-training is whether and when it is appropriate for individual mentoring to take place — that is, man to man or woman to woman.

We'll turn the table for a moment and pose that same question to you. When do you think it might be most beneficial to meet one on one with another husband? What issues would be appropriate to discuss apart from his spouse and yours? Write your thoughts here:

Truth be told, the need to meet one on one with a mentoree husband is rare. However, if you believe he is dealing with a particularly sensitive issue — perhaps an addiction, a sexual dysfunction, even an intense workplace or family situation that is affecting his marriage — or he approaches you privately about such a matter, and you feel you might be of assistance, you are certainly free to consult with him separately before directing him for further help.

ESSENTIAL SKILL TRAINING

Skill #1: Building Rapport
Skill #2: Walking in Another Couple's Shoes

Corresponds to chapters 8 – 9
of *The Complete Guide to Marriage Mentoring.*

This is the first of six sessions devoted to the actual skills you'll need as a marriage mentor. As you will soon see, these sessions will at times feel more like "self-exploration" than "training." That's for good reason. You can only take another couple where you have been yourselves. In fact, your self-awareness as a couple is one of the greatest tools you bring to this endeavor. So be prepared. You're going to get to know yourself, one another, and your marriage better as we proceed.

SKILL #1: BUILDING RAPPORT

"Dear Occupant."

Ever received a letter in the mail that begins this way? Of course! And what do you do? Get all excited to see what the letter has to say? If you're like most people, you toss it within seconds because you know that whoever wrote it doesn't even know you or care about you personally. What's missing? In a word, rapport.

You've used the word before. But what exactly does it mean?

Defining Rapport (5 MINUTES)

Write down any words that come to mind when you think of "rapport." Don't edit yourself.

_____   _____

_____   _____

_____   _____

_____   _____

Compare your descriptors with your spouse. And don't be alarmed if your wife is able to do this little assignment more quickly than you can. Research actually shows that women have more words in their vocabulary to describe something like rapport.

The dictionary defines *rapport* as "having a relationship characterized by harmony, accord, or affinity." If you study the origin of the term, you'll note that it comes from the word *port*, as in where a boat would find a safe harbor. And in a very real sense that's exactly what you are providing as marriage mentors.

But does this "safe harbor" just happen? Sometimes. We all have people we simply "click" with. But more often than not, rapport is something that develops. It takes some skill and intention on the part of the mentor to cultivate it.

Play the first DVD segment for session 4. (6 MINUTES)
Use the following space to take notes if you wish.

Now that you have witnessed a few real-life mentors and mentorees talking about the value of rapport, let's turn our attention to three ways you can build rapport with your own mentorees.

1. Identify with Your Mentorees

This is all about discovering what you have in common. And in a mentoring relationship it's not that tough. After all, whether you are mentoring a newlywed couple, a couple about to have a baby, a couple struggling with an addiction or debt or any other predicament, you are with them because of your similarities. For this reason, identifying with your mentoree couple normally should not require much work.

How Well Do You Identify? (6 MINUTES)

☕ One of the best ways to gauge your natural predilection for "identifying" is to ask for a reality check from your spouse, the person who knows you the best. Don't worry. This won't be as painful as you might imagine.

Choose a recent conversation in which you were listening to her talk about a situation that she found herself in (whether a traffic jam, a tough spot at work, a difficulty with a friend, etc.). Recall how you identified with her in that situation. For example, were you able to empathize? What feelings did you share with her? Note those thoughts/ remarks here:

☕ ☕ Now take turns getting your spouse's feedback on how well each of you thinks the other did "identifying" in the particular conversation. As you offer feedback, resist the urge to critique or defend; in other words, go easy on each other. Lower your guard, warm your heart, and learn what you can about your inclination to identify. Think of this exercise as simply holding up a mirror and thus raising your level of awareness.

2. Establish Credibility

Credibility is synonymous with believability or trustworthiness, defined by *Webster's Collegiate Dictionary* as "the quality or power of inspiring belief." Again, the very nature of your mentoring relationship will foster credibility. You've been where your mentorees are. You have experience. You know the ropes. So typically in the beginning stages of a mentoring relationship, you will have instant credibility. You will only lose that credibility if your mentorees begin to see you as untrustworthy or incompetent. Following is an exercise that will guard against that happening with your mentorees.

Staying Credible (9 MINUTES)

☕ Think of one of the most credible people you know. Write his or her name here:

_____

Now consider what makes this person credible in your eyes. Here are a number of qualities that may help direct your thinking. Circle the seven that you feel best apply.

Able	Intentional	Self-aware
Calm	Knowledgeable	Sensitive
Compassionate	Mature	Sincere
Confident	Observant	Skillful
Dependable	Organized	Stable
Educated	Principled	Tender
Focused	Questioning	Thoughtful
Giving	Rational	Trusting
Grounded	Realistic	Vulnerable
Helpful	Relaxed	Other: _____
Honest	Reliable	Other: _____

☕☕ Compare your list of qualities with that of your spouse. Did you choose any of the same qualities, even if you were describing different people?

Next, talk about these qualities that you both circled and how the *two of you* embody them or how you may need to cultivate them a bit more. Give each other feedback on each one. These qualities will be the ways your credibility comes through to your mentorees.

Finally, choose at least two credible qualities from the list that you both may need a little more of. How might you cultivate them to be more credible marriage mentors? Be specific.

3. Monitor Your Interest in Them

Have you ever been traveling in your car when you hear a good song on the radio, only the music begins to fade as you move out of signal range? You hear the song just enough to keep listening, but it becomes frustrating as the static distracts you from completely hearing the tune. That's exactly what monitoring your interest is about in the realm of marriage mentoring. It's about your ability to stay "tuned in" to your mentorees without becoming distracted.

Are You Distractible? (3 MINUTES)

How good are you at staying tuned in to a conversation? Does your mind wander more than most? Do you tend to interrupt and take the focus off the person speaking? Do you fight the urge to check your cell phone for sports scores or your BlackBerry for messages? Be honest.

   On the scale below, indicate your level of distractibility, on average, in most conversations.

Extremely Distractible   *Extremely Tuned In*

1   2   3   4   5   6   7   8   9   10

Now ask your spouse for feedback on your self-rating. Any surprises? By the way, as with most skills, you can learn to do this better. It just takes repeated practice.

SKILL #2: WALKING IN ANOTHER COUPLE'S SHOES

You can empathize without being a mentor, but you cannot mentor without empathy. It is difficult to exaggerate the importance of empathy to marriage mentoring. We believe that empathy is so vital to marriage mentoring that we often say your success in this endeavor will rise or fall based on how well you empathize with your mentorees. Without empathy, healthy relationships are impossible. Consider your contentment when another person senses what you are feeling without you having to say so. This is the essence of empathy.

   Often people confuse empathy with sympathy, but there's a difference. This next exercise will help you explore that very thing.

Empathy vs. Sympathy (5 MINUTES)

Do you know the difference? It's okay if you don't, but here's a chance to show off your knowledge if you do. Define each of these terms as best you can and give an example of each, as well.

Empathy is ...

_____

_____

_____

_____

Sympathy is ...

_____

_____

_____

_____

As always, compare your answers with your spouse and talk briefly about why you answered the way you did.

Empathy is deeper and stronger than sympathy. We've long used this analogy: Sympathy is standing on the shore and throwing out a lifeline to someone struggling in the water. Every decent human being—marriage mentor or not—sympathizes. It flows with the adrenaline. We barely have to think about it. Sympathy requires no training or skill. It's not terribly deliberate.

Empathy, on the other hand, is more daring, more deliberate. Empathy is jumping into the water and risking one's own safety to help a person who is struggling. And the risk is real. Why? Because empathy will change you. Once you empathize with someone, once you accurately understand what life must be like in their skin, you'll never see that person the same way again. You'll have more patience with them, more grace and compassion for them.

The difference between sympathy and empathy? Sympathy is all heart. Empathy involves both your head and your heart. It requires you to analyze as well as sympathize. It requires you to be both objective and subjective. That's the challenge of empathy.

Play the second DVD segment for session 4. (6 MINUTES)
Use the following space to take notes if you wish.

Now that you have heard from other real-life marriage mentors on the value and importance of empathy, let's take a look at how well you do this.

Assessing Your Empathy Quotient (15 MINUTES)

Following are twenty-four pairs of personal characteristics, or traits. For each pair, choose the trait that describes you more than it describes your partner. For instance, circle A if you are more "imaginative," or B if you value being "rational," as compared to your partner. Some of the traits will appear twice, but always in combination with a different trait. There are no right or wrong answers. Please be honest. And again, be sure you complete this assessment alone before talking about it with your spouse.

Compared to my partner, I am more...

A	B	1. imaginative – rational
A	B	2. helpful – quick-witted
A	B	3. neat – sympathetic
A	B	4. levelheaded – efficient
A	B	5. intelligent – considerate
A	B	6. self-reliant – ambitious
A	B	7. respectful – original
A	B	8. creative – sensible
A	B	9. generous – individualistic
A	B	10. responsible – original
A	B	11. capable – tolerant
A	B	12. trustworthy – wise
A	B	13. neat – logical
A	B	14. forgiving – gentle
A	B	15. efficient – respectful
A	B	16. practical – self-confident
A	B	17. capable – independent
A	B	18. alert – cooperative
A	B	19. imaginative – helpful
A	B	20. realistic – moral
A	B	21. considerate – wise
A	B	22. sympathetic – individualistic
A	B	23. ambitious – patient
A	B	24. reasonable – quick-witted

2. A	_____
3. B	_____
5. B	_____
7. A	_____
9. A	_____
11. B	_____
12. A	_____
14. A	_____
15. B	_____
18. B	_____
19. A	_____
20. B	_____
21. A	_____
22. A	_____
23. B	_____
Total	_____

Now take a moment to score the first part of this exercise. Give yourself a point for each answer that matches the key (above right). Note that items 1, 4, 6, 8, 10, 13, 16, 17, and 24 are "buffer" items and are not used in the scoring. There is a potential score of 0 to 15.

For part two of this exercise, answer each of the twenty questions by placing beside each of the statements the number that best describes you:

1 Rarely or none of the time
2 A little of the time
3 Some of the time
4 A good part of the time
5 Most or all of the time

1 2 3 4 5   1. When my partner and I have a disagreement, I win.

1 2 3 4 5   2. I'm more hard-driving than my partner.

1 2 3 4 5   3. I'm very good at solving problems for my partner.

1 2 3 4 5   4. Compared to my partner, I keep my feelings in check.

1 2 3 4 5   5. I'm good at accurately analyzing a situation or issue in our marriage.

1 2 3 4 5   6. I'm a natural problem solver.

1 2 3 4 5   7. Compared to my partner, I confront conflict head-on.

1 2 3 4 5   8. I'm assertive.

1 2 3 4 5   9. Relative to my partner, I'm more goal oriented.

1 2 3 4 5   10. I like to get to the facts more than my partner.

1 2 3 4 5   11. I have more "rules" about doing things than my partner.

1 2 3 4 5   12. I feel my partner is emotional.

1 2 3 4 5   13. I take control more than my partner does.

1 2 3 4 5   14. Compared to my partner, I would rather zero in on a solution than explore feelings.

1 2 3 4 5   15. I'm less sentimental than my partner.

1 2 3 4 5   16. I'm not easy to please because my expectations are high.

1 2 3 4 5   17. Compared to my partner, I'm more likely to criticize and pressure people to get things done.

1 2 3 4 5   18. I have no problem making my own needs known.

1 2 3 4 5   19. Compared to my partner, I'm less likely to show my emotions.

1 2 3 4 5   20. I want to be in control more than my partner does.

Score this self-test by totaling up your points on the items. There is a potential score of 20 to 100.

Total _____

The two parts of this exercise give you two subscores. The first half of the test reveals your "heart score" while the second half reveals your "head score." You can note them here:

Heart Score: _____   Head Score: _____

Making Sense of Your Head/Heart Self Test

As mentioned earlier, there are fifteen possible points on the Heart Talk test, indicating your inclination to sympathize. If you scored seven points or more, you are probably in the "high heart" zone. Below seven points puts you in the "low heart" zone. Note your score from the Heart Talk test on this continuum.

Low Heart Talk   *High Heart Talk*

0   7   15

There are 100 points on the Head Talk test, indicating your inclination to analyze. If you scored fifty or higher on this test, you are probably in the "high head" zone." Below fifty points puts you in the "low head" zone. Note your Head Talk score on this continuum.

Low Head Talk   *High Head Talk*

0   50   100

Now compare your scores with your partner. How do they differ? Is one of you more sympathetic (heart score) than the other? Is one of you more analytic (head score)? Chances are your scores are somewhat divergent. Typically, men emphasize the analytic aspect of empathy while women emphasize the sympathetic. Whether that's true in your relationship or not, the point is that you can work as a team to better empathize with your mentorees than either of you could by yourself.

AN OPTIONAL ASSIGNMENT: THE BIBLE AND EMPATHY

Does the New Testament say anything about empathy? Before the next session you may find it helpful to have the following Bible study with your spouse.

> NOTE: If you are doing this training in a group setting and can extend your session beyond sixty minutes, you might consider pairing up two or three couples to explore these passages together.

Meeting Another's Need

You won't find the word *empathy* in the New Testament, but the idea is captured strongly in the biblical word *compassion*. It's a natural response of Jesus to the suffering around him (see, for example, Matthew 9:36; 14:14; 20:34), a theme in parables such as the good Samaritan (Luke 10:33) and the prodigal son (Luke 15:20), and an ongoing command in the epistles (see Ephesians 4:32; Colossians 3:12; 1 John 3:17 – 18). The essence of New Testament compassion is recognition of and concern for another's need and appropriate action to meet that need. Look up any or all of the Bible references in this paragraph and discuss your findings with your spouse or the group, particularly as they affect your role of marriage mentor.

ESSENTIAL SKILL TRAINING

Skill #3: Working as a Team
Skill #4: Agreeing on Outcomes

Corresponds to chapters 10–11
of *The Complete Guide to Marriage Mentoring.*

Who can argue that marriage mentoring doesn't require teamwork? This skill is essential, as is knowing where you are headed together as a team. This session will show you how to use both of these skill sets to full advantage in your mentoring process.

SKILL #3: WORKING AS A TEAM

When it comes to marriage mentoring, it takes two leaders working in tandem. And that's not always an easy task. It requires some skill. Why? Because, one moment one of you may be taking the lead while the very next the other person will step in to focus direction. In other words, marriage mentoring requires passing the leadership baton back and forth, or more accurately, sharing it. You have to work as a team.

Here's an exercise to get you working in that direction.

What Makes You a Good Team? (5 MINUTES)

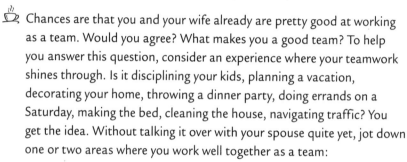 Chances are that you and your wife already are pretty good at working as a team. Would you agree? What makes you a good team? To help you answer this question, consider an experience where your teamwork shines through. Is it disciplining your kids, planning a vacation, decorating your home, throwing a dinner party, doing errands on a Saturday, making the bed, cleaning the house, navigating traffic? You get the idea. Without talking it over with your spouse quite yet, jot down one or two areas where you work well together as a team:

Next, and this may be a bit painful, note an area or two where you don't make the best teammates (and yes, every couple has these areas).

Now compare notes. What can you learn from your answers? Do you see your ability to work as a team in the same way? If not, what are the differences in your points of view? And, most importantly, what can you learn about your ability to work as a team from this exercise?

Play the first DVD segment for session 5. (6 MINUTES)
Use the following space to take notes if you wish.

Now that we've viewed the DVD segment, let's highlight three points that may help you ensure your teamwork as a marriage mentor couple: (1) understanding your unique strengths, (2) empowering each other's voice, and (3) embracing your differences.

1. Understanding Your Unique Strengths

As marriage mentors ourselves, I (Les) often found that I look to Leslie to bring closure to a conversation with our mentorees. She seems to have a knack for bringing everything together after a lengthy conversation and clarifying the next step. I (Leslie), on the other hand, know that Les feels more comfortable than I do in initiating a topic of conversation that might heighten anxiety.

What Are Your Individual Strengths as Mentors? (8 MINUTES)

Here's some feedback you're going to like. In this exercise we want you to discuss what each of you is good at in the area of mentoring. Granted, you may not have done much mentoring to this point, but you know your spouse well enough to know what strengths she will bring to the table.

So, without talking to her first, list four of her top interpersonal strengths right now.

My wife is great at . . .

1. _Listening - Empathy - honesty - not enabling_

Example: _____

2. _____

Example: _____

3. _____

Example: _____

4. _____

Example: _____

Now consider a specific example of how she has demonstrated each of the four strengths you just noted. The more specific the better.

Next, share your list of strengths with her and vice versa. The only rule for this part of the exercise is that the spouse hearing about their strengths can respond with only two words: *Thank you.* Why? Because we don't want you to use this time to downplay your strengths, qualify them, or explain them. For now, just hear what your partner has to say about what will make you a good mentor.

2. Empowering Each Other's Voice

As you watched the first DVD segment for this session, you saw how a tuning fork could represent your two voices as a marriage mentor team. It delivers a true pitch by two tines vibrating together. Muffle either side, even a little, and the note disappears. Neither individual tine produces the sweet, pure note. Only when both tines vibrate is the correct pitch heard.

How Do You Empower Each Other's Voice? (5 MINUTES)

When either one of your voices is muffled in the mentoring process, true marriage mentoring disappears. So consider how you can keep this from happening. Following are a couple of statements that you might hear your wife make in a typical mentoring session. In the space below each one, write a statement that you could make that would echo her point.

For example, if she says "Financial management is one of the key skills a couple can master to keep their home running smoothly," you can empower her voice by saying something as simple as: "That's exactly right." Or, "Not only is that true, but you practice what you preach when you say that."

You get the idea. Now try these out:

She says: "When a husband or wife takes a moment for a gentle caress or a tender touch, it's often more powerful than any spoken words."

You can empower her statement in front of your mentorees by saying:

She says: "I've always felt that marriage is never 50/50. If all I gave was half and that's all I expected from my spouse, we'd be in sad shape." You can empower her statement in front of your mentorees by saying:

Briefly compare answers with your spouse. You'll see that this technique is relatively easy to get the hang of and, we might add, a wonderful relationship builder apart from its positive effect in your mentoring role.

Another important way to empower each other's voices is to ask one another questions in front of your mentorees. For instance, it can be very helpful to turn to your partner in the course of your meeting and genuinely ask, "What do you think about what she's saying?" or "I bet you might have some thoughts on this issue." It's an invitation that shows your mentorees that you value each other's input.

3. Embracing Your Differences

Working together as a mentor team does not mean automatic agreement. Even as you empower each other's voice, you can certainly disagree. You have to be true to your own thinking and feeling. If your partner holds a different position than you do on parenting teenagers, for example, you need not stifle your opinion. In fact, your mentorees can learn much from watching the two of you successfully navigate your differences.

Navigating Your Differences (5 MINUTES)

Every couple has differences. And it's always helpful to know what differences might emerge between the two of you before they are exposed in front of your mentorees. In this exercise we simply want the two of you to rate, individually, how in sync you are on selected topics that sometimes can be points of difference in marriage.

	Different					Same
How much television to watch	1	2	3	4	5	6
Disciplining children	1	2	3	4	5	6
How we spend free time	1	2	3	4	5	6
Bringing work home from the office	1	2	3	4	5	6
How and when laundry should be done	1	2	3	4	5	6
What foods to eat	1	2	3	4	5	6
Whether to exercise	1	2	3	4	5	6
Where we go on vacation	1	2	3	4	5	6
How we relate to in-laws	1	2	3	4	5	6
When to turn off the cell phone	1	2	3	4	5	6
How to drive a car	1	2	3	4	5	6
Whether to have a pet	1	2	3	4	5	6
How to celebrate Christmas	1	2	3	4	5	6

After you compare your rankings with your spouse, explore how you might handle issues you differ about and any others that could emerge in a mentoring session. In other words, how will you embrace your differences and still function as a team? What will your mentorees learn from seeing how you handle differences?

SKILL #4: AGREEING ON OUTCOMES

What does it mean to agree on outcomes? It means being proactive about where you'd like to be as two couples in a mentoring relationship when you have completed your work. It means getting specific and charting your course.

Agreeing on outcomes, however, is not always easy. It requires initiative. It requires your mentorees to take responsibility for their marriage. After all, you can't do the work for them. You are mentors, not mothers. Make no mistake, your mentorees will never achieve their ideal marriage as mere passengers; they must have their collective hand on the wheel and agree with you on some specific outcomes.

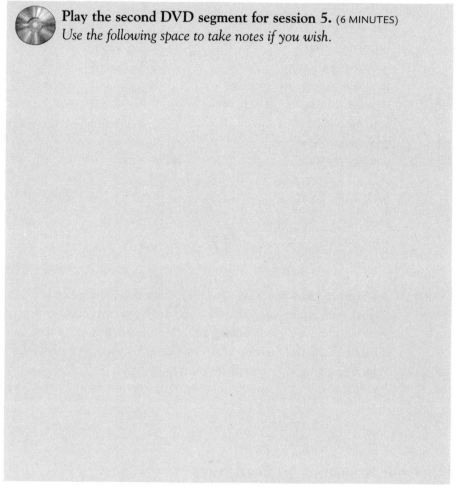

Play the second DVD segment for session 5. (6 MINUTES)
Use the following space to take notes if you wish.

In *The Complete Guide to Marriage Mentoring*, we provide several practical ways you can come to agree on outcomes. We'll highlight four of them for you to interact with in this training module.

1. "If You Could Press a Magic Button ..."

Here's a question we've probably asked every couple we've ever mentored: *If you could press a magic button, what would you like to instantly make different in your marriage?* If they are stuck, we may give them some suggestions. Perhaps they'd like to enjoy more romance. Maybe they'd like to have fewer quarrels. Would they prefer to have more meals as a family with the television off? Every couple has things they'd like to change, and this question will serve as a springboard for setting goals that will help them improve their relationship.

Ready for a Little Magic? (6 MINUTES)

Here's an exercise you can do with your mentorees. We'll have you do it yourself so you can see how it works.

Make a list of three or four things you wish were different in your marriage. Do this separately before comparing notes. Write your "wish list" here:

1. _____

_____

2. _____

_____

3. _____

_____

4. _____

_____

After you compare your lists with your spouse, try to prioritize the top two items you would change about your marriage if you could press a magic button.

2. Set Objective and Attainable Goals

Obviously, this is something you want to do early on with any mentoree couple. Knowing your objectives gives everyone a purpose and a sense of comfort. It provides direction for you *and* your mentorees. And truth be told, they probably haven't thought much about their goals. Most couples don't. Only a small fraction have ever put their goals in writing. How about you?

Where Are You Going? (9 MINUTES)

You knew it was coming. So let's get straight to it. Write down the goals you have for your marriage — and in this exercise you can feel free to talk about it together before you write your answer.

In the next month we intend to . . .

_____

_____

_____

In the next twelve months we intend to . . .

_____

_____

_____

In the next five years we intend to . . .

_____

_____

_____

Research reveals that simply having a list of goals in your possession dramatically increases your chances of reaching those goals. Not only that, people who make a tangible list and keep it handy are far more likely to achieve their goals than others who have the very same desires.

Whether you are mentoring an engaged couple, a couple wanting to move from good to great, or a couple in distress, take time early on to discuss their goals. Write them down. Have them do the same. Decide on a place where they can keep them visible. Both partners need to see them several times throughout the week.

3. Be Sure the Goals Align with God's Purpose

In *The Complete Guide to Marriage Mentoring*, we tell the story of how Matt Emmons lost out on what seemed a sure gold medal at the 2004 Olympic 50-meter three-position rifle event. He didn't even need a bull's-eye to win. His final shot merely needed to be on target. But Emmons lost because he fired at the wrong target. His score for a good shot at the wrong target? Zero. Instead of a medal, Emmons ended up in eighth place.

The point? It doesn't matter how accurate you are if you are aiming at the wrong goal. As you help your mentorees craft their goals for their marriage, be sure to seek God's guidance. Pray together as couples that this goal-setting process would honor Christ. Pray that God would reveal his desires during this time you share together. Never make them feel guilty for their goals, but help them consider how their goals align with God's purpose for their lives together.

Rather than providing you with an interactive exercise for this point, we simply suggest that each of you pray for wisdom and guidance in this area — even before you meet your mentorees.

4. Get Specific on What You Can Commit To

Let's get to one of the nitty-gritty aspects of marriage mentoring. You only have so much time to devote to this ministry given your many other commitments. So what are your limits? How many hours per month are you willing to give?

Setting Your Personal Boundaries as a Couple (5 MINUTES)

This, of course, is a discussion for just the two of you to explore — before you meet with your mentorees and sometimes even after you get to know them. Here's the topic: What are we willing to give?

Why talk about this here? Because it may influence the kind of goals you will set with your mentorees. So be honest with each other and set your limits right from the beginning. Take five minutes to answer these questions together as best you can right now:

- How often can you meet with your mentorees?

- When can you meet with your mentorees?

- Do you want to meet with them in your own home? In their home?

- Would you rather meet over a meal at a quiet restaurant?

- For how many sessions can you meet?

- Do you want to be finished by a certain date?

The more specific you can be about what you would like the structure of this time to look like, the better. Why? Because then you can let your mentorees know the boundaries. You'll avoid any unspoken disappointment—on your side as well as theirs.

ESSENTIAL SKILL TRAINING

Skill #5: Asking Meaningful Questions
Skill #6: Listening Aggressively

Corresponds to chapters 12–13
of *The Complete Guide to Marriage Mentoring.*

English philosopher Francis Bacon said, "A prudent question is one-half of wisdom." We believe this is especially true for marriage mentors. And we might add that the second half of wisdom is *listening* "aggressively" to how your mentorees answer questions. In this training session you'll delve into both skills. And, as always, we will help you explore your own marriage as a means to honing them.

SKILL #5: ASKING MEANINGFUL QUESTIONS

Most people never learn the art of asking a good question. They simply pose a query if it happens to pop into their head. Not so for a marriage mentor who has discovered the power of a good question. They don't take this skill for granted. A meaningful question is as important to an effective marriage mentor as a scalpel is to a surgeon.

Before viewing the DVD segment on this topic, consider the ingredients that go into asking a good question by doing the following exercise.

What Makes a Question Meaningful? (3 MINUTES)

Take a minute to complete this sentence-stem on your own:

A meaningful question . . .

_____

_____

_____

Now discuss your definition with your spouse. Were your answers similar? Do you agree with each other? Why or why not?

Play the first DVD segment for session 6. (6 MINUTES)
Use the following space to take notes if you wish.

Now that you know what we mean by a "meaningful question" and have heard from some real-life mentor and mentoree couples, it's your turn to start crafting meaningful questions that you could pose to a mentoree couple.

We're going to start by giving you an exercise to help you explore your current level of question-asking competency, after which there will be an interactive exercise to help you refine the skill. Here's the first exercise.

How Well Do You Ask Meaningful Questions? (8 MINUTES)

You just saw on the video that a meaningful question invites vulnerability, but is not invasive. It is personal, but respects privacy. It is genuine, but not blunt. So how would you rate yourself at posing these kinds of questions in your conversations? Review your past week and the conversations you've had at work, with friends, and in your family. How well did you do in each category?

This week, when it came to posing meaningful questions to people, I would say I did this...

At Work

Not so well   *Very well*

1   2   3   4   5   6   7   8   9   10

If you ranked yourself 5 or higher, note a specific example from your week:

With Friends

Not so well   *Very well*

1   2   3   4   5   6   7   8   9   10

If you ranked yourself 5 or higher, note a specific example from your week:

At Home

Not so well   *Very well*

1   2   3   4   5   6   7   8   9   10

If you ranked yourself 5 or higher, note a specific example from your week:

Now share your answers with your spouse. Ask for genuine feedback. Approach this as a real learning opportunity and help each other, as iron sharpens iron, to more accurately measure your personal effectiveness at this question-asking skill.

Whether you are already an "old pro" at the fine art of question-asking or realize you still have a long way to go, this next exercise is another excellent activity for practicing this skill.

Practice What You Ask (15 MINUTES)

The best way to help you craft meaningful questions is to practice on each other. If you are using this training manual in a group setting, we recommend that you do this exercise couple to couple—taking turns role-playing mentors and mentorees. If you are training as husband and wife in an individual setting, you will still benefit from this exercise. You'll simply interact one on one.

Here's what you do. As a couple (or as an individual spouse if not in a group), quickly select two topics that may typically come up in a mentoring situation, for example: household chores, free time, disciplining children, communication, in-laws, balancing work demands, handling emotions, personality differences, goal setting. Write each of those selected topics in the space provided below. Next, write a meaningful question or two about each topic that you might pose to mentorees. Be sure that these are questions you yourself would be comfortable answering, because in a real-life situation your mentorees may very well turn a question back in your direction.

Topic #1: _____

Question: _____

Question: _____

Topic #2: _____

Question: _____

Question: _____

Now you are ready to practice. If you're doing this with another couple, find out whose wedding anniversary date is coming up sooner. They will be the first to ask their questions as you play the part of the mentorees. After about five minutes, switch roles and ask your questions of them.

The key to making this exercise work is to be genuine. Don't simply blurt out your questions to check them off your list. Use them conversationally to draw out responses from the other couple. Of course, this will feel artificial. That's to be expected. The point is to learn to work together as a couple while putting the spotlight on another couple.

NOTE: Jesus was masterful at asking meaningful questions. Page 133 of *The Complete Guide to Marriage Mentoring* features a chart with a number of those question-asking situations and the corresponding Scripture passages. You and your spouse may want to study these at some point.

SKILL #6: LISTENING AGGRESSIVELY

Your ears are very persuasive. Did you know that? You can often influence your mentorees just as much by how you listen as by what you say. And in this portion of your training session we intend to help your ears become as persuasive as possible.

Before viewing the DVD segment for this skill, here's a little exercise to get you and your ears warmed up.

Why Are Your Ears Most Likely to Be Persuasive? (3 MINUTES)

Most people readily admit that it's easier to listen on some occasions than it is on others. What makes the difference for you?

Following is a list of the six most common barriers to effective listening. Rank order 1 – 6 how much each one of these is likely to keep you from listening the way you'd like (1 being the most likely to keep you from listening well to your mentorees).

_____ *Distractions* — Telephone, television, pager, and all the rest.

_____ *Defensiveness* — Perceiving a comment as a criticism.

_____ *Closed-mindedness* — Not being open to other's opinions and ideas.

_____ *Projection* — Attributing your own thoughts and feelings to another person (believing "he's the one who's angry," when you're the one hot under the collar).

_____ *Assumption* — Drawing conclusions about the meaning or intention of what is said before you truly understand it.

_____ *Pride* — Thinking you have little to learn from the other person.

Now ask your spouse for feedback on how you ranked these. See what you can learn about yourself as a listener from your soul mate.

Play the second DVD segment for session 6. (6 MINUTES)
Use the following space to take notes if you wish.

You've just seen how valuable listening can be in the marriage mentoring process. In the remainder of this session we provide you with an exercise designed to help you internalize and practice the points you have just observed.

Listening with the Third Ear (15 MINUTES)

One of the most important aspects of listening that you will bring into a mentoring relationship is "reflecting feelings" — when you listen not just to the words that your mentorees are using but to the emotional message beneath them.

If you are doing this exercise in a group setting, you will once again pair up with another couple. Each will take turns: one couple interacting while the other couple observes and later debriefs with feedback. If you are doing this exercise one on one, you will simply "critique" each other.

Below are two sample statements a wife might make to her husband, each followed by a potential reflective comment he might offer in return.

SHE: "You are always so eager to solve my problem but sometimes I don't want a solution."

HE: "Sounds like you just want to be understood."

SHE: "Just once I'd like not to have to pick up everybody's clothes off the floor."

HE: "That's got to be aggravating."

Now it's time for you and your spouse to practice. She will read three "wife" statements from her manual, to which you must respond reflectively. You will read the following three "husband" statements to her, and she must respond reflectively as well.

1. "I can't believe you agreed to volunteer us for something without asking me first."
2. "Why can't you get ready at the same time I do? It seems like I'm always waiting on you."
3. "Everyone at work seems to be moving up the proverbial ladder but me."

By the way, though there are no "right or wrong" answers, here are potential reflective comments she might make to these statements:

1. "Sounds like you are feeling trapped." Or, "Sounds like you are feeling betrayed."
2. "You sound frustrated. I appreciate you being so patient."
3. "You must feel like you're getting passed over."

While the two of you trade statements and reflective comments back and forth, the other couple (if you are in a group setting) simply observes; their role is to learn by watching. You will do the same with them as soon as you finish. As former baseball star Yogi Berra, a master of stating the obvious, once said, "You can see a lot by just watching." Once you're all done, both couples should debrief on how easy or difficult this skill is for them, and together answer the following questions:

- Do you agree that reflecting feelings is an important part of active listening with mentorees? Why or why not?

- What do you predict will be your biggest challenge as a couple when it comes to reflecting another couple's feelings? What can you do to overcome it?

Chapter 13 in *The Complete Guide to Marriage Mentoring* goes more in-depth on the topic of active listening.

ESSENTIAL SKILL TRAINING

Skill #7: Fielding Questions
Skill #8: Telling Your Stories

Corresponds to chapters 14–15
of *The Complete Guide to Marriage Mentoring.*

Each of the skills you are learning in this training series builds on one another. And when it comes to fielding questions and telling your stories, you'll certainly rely on each of the skills we've covered—from building rapport to listening aggressively. So let's jump into this new skill set.

SKILL #7: FIELDING QUESTIONS

One of the most anxiety-provoking aspects of marriage mentoring for some mentor couples is the fear of being asked a question that they can't answer. In fact, the anxiety we sometimes felt in training marriage mentors years ago led us to write *Questions Couples Ask*, a book containing answers to the top 100 questions married couples ask. One marriage mentor couple told us it had become their security blanket because they knew they had a place to start when they were stymied.

Truth be told, you don't need that book to feel secure when it comes to fielding your mentorees' questions. This session is designed to boost your confidence by showing you how to handle any question they throw at you.

Before playing the DVD segment for this skill, we want you to get your mind engaged with the topic by way of a brief exercise.

What Could They Ask? (4 MINUTES)

As you imagine potential mentoring meetings, what could mentorees ask that might give you pause? Is it a question about financial management? Sex? Your own in-law situation? Following is a list of potential topics that may come up in any given marriage mentoring relationship. Rate your anxiety level for each:

Questions about Communicating Better

Feeling Secure   *Feeling Anxious*

Questions about Resolving Arguments and Conflict

Feeling Secure   *Feeling Anxious*

Questions about Handling Emotions like Anger or Resentment

Feeling Secure   *Feeling Anxious*

1   2   3   4   5   6   7   8   9   10

Questions about Career Directions and Charting a Future

Feeling Secure   *Feeling Anxious*

Questions about the Differences Between the Genders

Feeling Secure   *Feeling Anxious*

1 ——— 2 ——— 3 ——— 4 ——— 5 ——— 6 ——— 7 ——— 8 ——— 9 ——— 10

Questions about In-Law Issues

Feeling Secure   *Feeling Anxious*

1 ——— 2 ——— 3 ——— 4 ——— 5 ——— 6 ——— 7 ——— 8 ——— 9 ——— 10

Questions about Money Management and Debt

Feeling Secure   *Feeling Anxious*

1 ——— 2 ——— 3 ——— 4 ——— 5 ——— 6 ——— 7 ——— 8 ——— 9 ——— 10

Questions about Sexual Issues

Feeling Secure   *Feeling Anxious*

1 ——— 2 ——— 3 ——— 4 ——— 5 ——— 6 ——— 7 ——— 8 ——— 9 ——— 10

Questions about Spiritual Matters

Feeling Secure   *Feeling Anxious*

1 ——— 2 ——— 3 ——— 4 ——— 5 ——— 6 ——— 7 ——— 8 ——— 9 ——— 10

Questions about Parenting and Discipline Issues

Feeling Secure   *Feeling Anxious*

1 ——— 2 ——— 3 ——— 4 ——— 5 ——— 6 ——— 7 ——— 8 ——— 9 ——— 10

Questions about Your Own Marriage Relationship

Feeling Secure   *Feeling Anxious*

1 ——— 2 ——— 3 ——— 4 ——— 5 ——— 6 ——— 7 ——— 8 ——— 9 ——— 10

Now review your rankings and note the one or two areas about which you feel most anxious. By the way, if you're not feeling anxious about any of these issues, that may be a sign that you're denying the real anxiety you feel about this process. If that's the case, you may want to take anther stab at it.

 Share with your spouse the areas about which you feel most anxious. Do you have any in common?

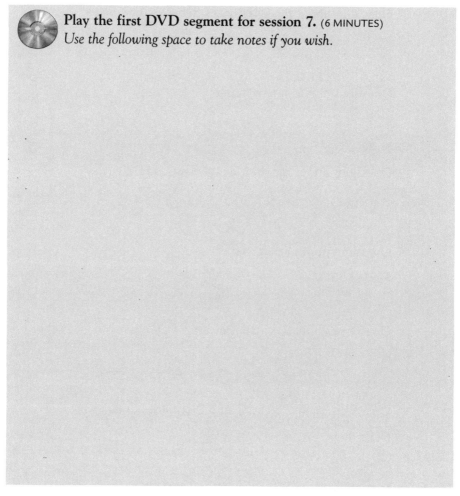

Play the first DVD segment for session 7. (6 MINUTES)
Use the following space to take notes if you wish.

You've now seen that real-life mentor couples can handle a myriad of questions and live to talk about it. This is not an area that need cause undue anxiety or concern. In this training session we want you to have some fun with the following exercise.

Stump the Couple (10 MINUTES)

If you are using this manual in a group setting, connect with another couple for this role-playing exercise. If you are doing this training as an individual couple, you can still do this exercise with each other (simply modify the steps below or find another couple who would be willing to role-play as mentorees with you).

First, as a couple, pretend you are mentorees and select a topic of conversation you'd like to explore with your "mentors" (the other couple). It may be helpful to make your topic one that causes you anxiety (perhaps the one that topped both of your lists from the previous exercise). But any realistic topic will do.

Now, follow the steps below:

1. Choose which couple will go first as the mentors. The other couple will role-play being mentorees.
2. The mentorees begin talking about their topic and the mentors interact as realistically as possible.
3. The mentorees then get around to asking a question — one that might not necessarily be easy.
4. The mentors proceed to handle the question just as they would if it were an actual mentoring session.
5. After two or three minutes, reverse roles so the other couple gets an opportunity to ask their "tough question."

Once finished, take a few more minutes to debrief. Consider:

- How did you feel you and your spouse did handling the other couple's question?
- What worked and what didn't?
- Were you able to "reflect the feeling" behind the question (as you learned in the previous session) to ensure the mentorees' question was understood?

As you debrief your role plays, consider the motive behind the question. Do you think their question could have been a means to avoid doing something they already knew to do? Could one partner have been looking for an ally in the mentors to support their position? Or do you think they were legitimately looking for help?

SKILL #8: TELLING YOUR STORIES

We now turn our attention to a skill that you might consider using as you field a question from your mentorees. As we've discovered, mentors can often answer almost any question with a story. Before you watch the DVD segment on this skill, complete this exercise.

Once Upon a Time (5 MINUTES)

Everyone has a favorite childhood story, one that we've heard, read, or seen often and still fondly remember. It may be *The Three Little Pigs*, *Charlotte's Web*, *The Little Engine That Could*, *The Wizard of Oz*, *Peter Pan*, or *Huckleberry Finn*. The list goes on and on.

Write the name of a favorite childhood story plus a couple of specific reasons why it still stays with you:

One of my favorite stories is: _____

The reasons are:

1._____

2._____

Now, briefly talk about your choice with your spouse. Could you have predicted what each of you chose?

Also surmise why stories—telling them and hearing them from others—is important . . . especially as it relates to marriage mentoring. What do you think stories, particularly your own stories, might do for a marriage mentoree couple?

Play the second DVD segment for session 7. (6 MINUTES)
Use the following space to take notes if you wish.

If there is one thing you now know, after watching this DVD segment, it's that storytelling in a marriage mentoring session requires mentors to be vulnerable. Of course, there's more to it than vulnerability but such transparency is essential.

Before we ask you to practice your storytelling, here's a summary of important points to keep in mind as you learn to tell your stories together:

As a marriage mentor, you tell a good story when you ...

- Relate to your mentorees something personal about your own marriage relationship.

- Keep in mind that your story is not about you. It's about your mentorees.

- Poke fun at yourself. Your mentorees will enjoy knowing that you're not perfect.

- Tell them sparingly. While storytelling is essential to marriage mentoring, it's not the goal.

- Your stories are spontaneous and relevant to what you are discussing.

- You both tell a story together, freely interrupting each other to be sure your mentorees see both sides.

- You also provide space and a listening ear to hear your mentorees' stories.

Telling Your Stories (20 MINUTES)

While some stories are purely for entertainment, most of your stories should convey a point. You don't want your mentorees to walk away saying, "What was that about?" but rather, "That story reminds me of us; maybe we should do the same thing." Or, "That story was powerful; I want to be sure we don't make the same mistake."

To ensure that this happens, this exercise provides opportunity to practice telling your story with intentionality. Ideally, it requires another couple besides yourselves. If you are in a group setting, that's easy enough. If you are doing this training in an individual setting, recruit another couple to help you out.

Before you connect with another couple, consider with your spouse your own stories. In other words, note any humorous, poignant, meaningful, painful, life-changing, or otherwise interesting story that relates to marriage—and probably to other couples. We all have them. They are what make our marriage what it is.

Take two or three minutes right now to jot a reminder of a few of these stories from your marital odyssey.

_____

_____

_____

_____

Here's the fun part. Join with another couple and take about five minutes apiece to tell one of your stories (obviously there's no time limit if you're doing this exercise outside a group setting). This may be a story you have already told. That's okay. Simply focus on sharing the story together and what its point might be if told in a mentoring context. Ask the other couple if they have suggestions on how the two of you could improve your storytelling or what particular mentoring value they see in your story.

ESSENTIAL SKILL TRAINING

Skill #9: Praying Together
Skill #10: Staying Sharp

Corresponds to chapters 16 – 17
of *The Complete Guide to Marriage Mentoring.*

If ever two skills went together in this manual, it's these. For how can you stay sharp together without prayer? This session will help you explore these two important aspects of marriage mentoring — to ensure you are the sharpest instruments in God's hands that you can be.

SKILL #9: PRAYING TOGETHER

We recently saw a cartoon of two praying mantises looking at each other. The caption read, "Sure, everyone thinks we're praying, but do any of us actually make the time for it?"

Can you identify? Do you ever feel guilty for not praying more often? If you're like most believers, you probably do. But don't worry, this session is not about sending you on a guilt trip. Far from it. We want to free you from the "obligation" of prayer and demonstrate the great "opportunity" it provides to your mentoring relationship.

As usual, here's an exercise to do before watching the DVD segment.

Is Prayer Your Steering Wheel or Your Spare Tire? (4 MINUTES)

Corrie ten Boom once asked this title question. And it's a good one. How would *you* answer? We want to give you a moment to do just that. But first consider that our prayer lives are typically shaped by past influences, including the homes in which we grew up. That's one of the reasons that everyone prays a little differently—for different reasons at different times in different ways.

Briefly discuss with your spouse each of the following questions:

- Did your mom and dad pray together?
- How would you describe your personal prayer life?
- Do you ever feel like you treat prayer as a spare tire (only for emergencies) instead of a steering wheel (the guiding power of your life)?
- How do you feel about praying with your mentorees?

Whether you are a prayer warrior or not, whether you look forward to praying with another couple or it scares you silly, this session will help you get a handle on prayer and show you how to use it as a "steering wheel" with your mentorees.

Play the first DVD segment for session 8. (6 MINUTES)
Use the following space to take notes if you wish.

You've probably heard or read the following Scripture verse many times but it bears repeating: "Where two or three come together in my name, there am I with them" (Matthew 18:20). This promise is just too valuable not to bring into the marriage mentoring relationship. And, by the way, you don't have to be a prayer warrior or a "giant of the faith" to pray. As long a you are taking time for prayer, you can be assured that God will make himself present.

For this reason alone, prayer is a significant tool for every marriage mentor. And this exercise will help you use it more effectively.

Praying for Your Mentorees (10 MINUTES)

Intercession is defined as a petition to God on behalf of another. And it is vital to an effective marriage mentoring relationship. "Intercession is the link between man's impotence and God's omnipotence," said the noted nineteenth-century pastor Andrew Murray.

In John 16:6 – 24, Christ prayed for his disciples, and in the same way we can pray for our mentorees. This exercise is more of a mini Bible study on intercessory prayer. After all, there is no one right way of doing this. The important thing is simply to pray.

You already know that Scripture *urges* us to pray for others. With your spouse, read aloud the following verses, then go back and circle any of the words that you believe can guide you in how to pray for your mentorees.

> *Pray in the Spirit on all occasions with all kinds of prayers and requests. With this in mind, be alert and always keep on praying for all the saints.*
>
> EPHESIANS 6:18

> *I urge, then, first of all, that requests, prayers, intercession and thanksgiving be made for everyone.... This is good, and pleases God our Savior.*
>
> 1 TIMOTHY 2:1 – 3

Record any thoughts from your brief study of these two passages (especially as it pertains to "requests").

We are also given *examples* of praying for others. Again, with your spouse, read aloud the following verses and circle any of the words that you believe can guide you in how to pray for your mentorees. Afterward, record any additional thoughts you have on how these passages might inform your intercessions.

Epaphras, who is one of you and a servant of Christ Jesus, sends greetings. He is always wrestling in prayer for you, that you may stand firm in all the will of God, mature and fully assured.

COLOSSIANS 4:12

I have not stopped giving thanks for you, remembering you in my prayers. I keep asking that the God of our Lord Jesus Christ, the glorious Father, may give you the Spirit of wisdom and revelation, so that you may know him better. I pray also that the eyes of your heart may be enlightened in order that you may know the hope to which he has called you, the riches of his glorious inheritance in the saints, and his incomparably great power for us who believe.

EPHESIANS 1:16 – 19

I pray that you, being rooted and established in love, may have power, together with all the saints, to grasp how wide and long and high and deep is the love of Christ, and to know this love that surpasses knowledge — that you may be filled to the measure of all the fullness of God.

EPHESIANS 3:17 – 19

Praying with Your Mentorees

Some people feel uncomfortable about praying aloud with others. This isn't an indication of their spiritual maturity or fervor. It typically has more to do with how they are hardwired for social interactions. If you fall into this category, don't worry. We aren't going to force you to pray with your mentorees if that makes you uncomfortable. Be we can tell you that if you do pray with your mentorees you — and they — are very likely to find it rewarding. Here's an exercise to help you explore doing just that.

Do You Pray What I Pray? (6 MINUTES)

First of all, let's take a quick look at your comfort level when it comes to praying with your mentorees, couple to couple. Be honest and rate yourself on this continuum:

Quite Uncomfortable   *Eager to Do So*

1   2   3   4   5   6   7   8   9   10

Talk about your self-rating with your spouse. Why do you feel the way you do? Remember, there is no "right" ranking. This is simply a time of honest sharing about your comfort level with public prayer in this setting.

Now, if you are willing, consider how you might most effectively pray with your mentorees. Typically this is done near the end of a mentoring session (though it can certainly take place at any time) when you simply ask them: "Can we pray together?"

So take it from there. What considerations are important to you and your spouse in this process? For example, you may want to ensure that your mentorees don't feel obligated to pray aloud with you (avoiding guilt motivation). Note those considerations here as you discuss them with your spouse.

Whether mentorees choose to pray aloud or not, you can wrap up the session by letting them know that you'll pray for them in the coming days. Ask them to answer the following three questions so that you might pray with their responses in mind:

1. As you review this past week, what are you most thankful for in your partner?
2. What's a pressure point the two of you are likely to encounter in your upcoming week?

3. What's one positive and concrete action for improving your marriage that you'd like to take this week?

Talk briefly with your spouse as to whether these questions might work for your style as a couple. Why or why not?

SKILL #10: STAYING SHARP

The most important tool you have as a mentor couple is your own marriage. It's difficult to exaggerate this point. Who you are — both individually and as a couple — is the most powerful "lesson" you will ever teach your mentorees. That's why this skill set focuses on you.

Before viewing the next DVD segment, complete this brief self-test.

Getting to Know You (5 MINUTES)

The following true-false questions are designed to raise your awareness about several self-dimensions. Of course, it's rare for any of these characteristics to be completely true or completely false, but circle the response that *best* describes you. You won't be sharing your answers with anyone but your spouse.

T	F	I manage my emotions well.
T	F	I'm known for being able to see issues from other people's perspectives.
T	F	I feel at ease and confident most of the time.
T	F	Most people would say I listen attentively.
T	F	I'm willing to be vulnerable about my weaknesses.
T	F	I withhold judgment until I have time to formulate a valid opinion.
T	F	I'm basically trusting of other people.
T	F	I have the courage to confront a challenge.
T	F	I take time to consistently and intentionally renew my spirit.

Compare your answers with your spouse's. Which of your answers most surprised your spouse and why? Which of those statements that you answered "false" would you most like to work on and why?

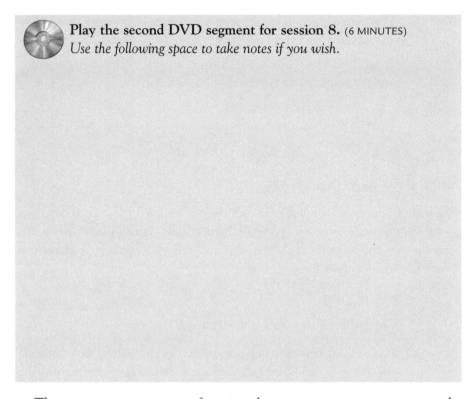

Play the second DVD segment for session 8. (6 MINUTES)
Use the following space to take notes if you wish.

There are numerous ways of staying sharp as a marriage mentor couple. You saw in the DVD segment how many couples do this. And chances are that you are already doing many things that renew the spirit of your marriage. The following exercise focuses on one way of staying sharp and renewing your spirits that you may have overlooked.

Enjoying the Rare Delicacy of Slow Food (5 MINUTES)

A telltale sign of a frazzled marriage is mealtime madness. Whether these couples catch their food on the go, multitask during the meal (read, watch TV, or talk on the phone), or have to serve or referee a tableful of kids, they rarely take time to linger, and thus miss an important opportunity to recharge their marital batteries. So let's consider how you might begin to make mealtime more meaningful.

Some couples find it enjoyable to cook together. We're not one of them. But we do enjoy a slow-paced meal. For us, that unhurried meal is typically at a quiet restaurant. Every couple finds their own way to share a slow meal. This exercise is designed to get the two of you talking about it. There are no right or wrong answers, just questions to discuss.

1. When would you say was the last time the two of you had a slow-paced meal with no television or other distractions?

   ☐ This week
   ☐ This month
   ☐ This year
   ☐ Can't remember

2. How prone are you to sabotage a potential slow-paced meal by replacing it with fast food?

   ☐ Most days
   ☐ At least once a week
   ☐ Once or twice a month
   ☐ Almost never

3. If you are prone to fast food, why would you say you are most likely to indulge?

   ☐ It's cheap.
   ☐ It's fast.
   ☐ It's easy.
   ☐ It's fun (for the kids).

4. Would you like to have more slow-paced meals together or are you doing well in this area already? Why or why not?

5. When would the two of you be most likely to enjoy a slow-paced meal together? Is there a certain day of the week that works best?

6. What's your favorite part of having an unhurried mealtime together?

Before leaving this session on staying sharp as a marriage mentor couple, we want to remind you of an important aspect of your relationship that can make a tremendous difference. Complete the following exercise on your own.

Making Your Mundane Moments Count (4 MINUTES)

What can you do to prepare your mind for the little but important moments that make up every day in every marriage? Below is a list of common moments, times when we are likely to connect with each other as spouses. They also are times that too often slip right by even the most dedicated marriage mentors without much thought or intention. Consider each item and rate how well you do it.

Saying good morning as you start your day ...

Saying thanks for the common things each day ...

Saying I understand ...

Saying I love you ...

Saying hello when you greet each other at the end of a workday ...

Now, review those items you ranked 4 or less. What can you do to be more mindful of these common moments? In other words, how can you become more invested and present in each of them? By doing so, by giving them some forethought, you're much more likely to make them meaningful when they happen. Choose two items and focus on them in the week ahead. See if your spouse notices a difference.

ESSENTIAL SKILL TRAINING

Skill #11: Being Yourself and Going with the Flow
Bonus Skill: Spotting Red Flags

Corresponds to chapter 18 and appendix 8
of *The Complete Guide to Marriage Mentoring.*

We come to the final skill training session of being yourself and going with the flow. Before we jump into it, let's quickly review. We've talked about ...

- Building rapport and walking in another couple's shoes
- Working as a team and agreeing on outcomes
- Asking meaningful questions and listening aggressively
- Fielding questions and telling your stories
- Praying together and staying sharp

This final skill set is designed to help you take all of these other skills and make them your own. After all, there are as many different styles of marriage mentoring as there are marriage mentors.

SKILL #11: BEING YOURSELF AND GOING WITH THE FLOW

Ready to get real? That's what "being yourself and going with the flow" is all about. Authenticity. To help you dial into this topic that you are about to explore on the DVD segment, complete this brief exercise.

Let's Get Real (5 MINUTES)

 Who is the most authentic, genuine, real person you know? Your spouse or another close family member is excluded from the running. Consider someone who you know now or have known in the past. It may be someone who you haven't even met, but perceive to be especially real. Write the person's name here:

One of the most authentic people I know is . . .

_____

Now consider what makes this person authentic in your eyes. And share this with your spouse. What is it about them that makes you feel they are so genuine?

Play the DVD segment for session 9. (8 MINUTES)
Use the following space to take notes if you wish.

All of us have a built-in radar detector for phoniness. Your mentorees are no exception. So what can you do to ensure that you will be yourselves — the real deal — as you mentor them? This exercise will help.

Taking Off Your Masks (10 MINUTES)

 The primary reason some people don't seem genuine is because they are wearing an interpersonal mask. Think about it. Each of us has a natural, built-in desire to be known, but we often stifle our vulnerability out of fear. We're afraid of being seen as too emotional or not emotional enough, as too assertive or not assertive enough, too whatever or not whatever enough. We're afraid of rejection.

The result? We wear masks. We put up our guard. We become what some have called "jellyfish in armor" by pretending to be, think, or feel something we aren't. Of course, all of us wear social masks (acting calm or confident when we're not) from time to time.

This exercise will help you discover just what your masks look like and when you are most likely to wear them to avoid feeling judged or perceived negatively. It focuses on three areas: work, home, and church; if you'd like to substitute an area that is more appropriate to your situation, feel free.

I wear masks at work:

Very Often   *Almost Never*

1   2   3   4   5   6   7

If your answer was between 1 and 4, describe the kinds of masks you wear at work and with whom.

I wear masks at home:

Very Often   *Almost Never*

1   2   3   4   5   6   7

If your answer was between 1 and 4, describe the kinds of masks you wear at home and with whom.

I wear masks at church:

Very Often   *Almost Never*

1   2   3   4   5   6   7

If your answer was between 1 and 4, describe the kinds of masks you wear at church and with whom.

Now review your responses with your spouse and determine which of your masks serves a helpful function and which may be interfering with your ability to cultivate healthy relationships. What can you do to discard these unhealthy masks?

BONUS SKILL: SPOTTING RED FLAGS

Before leaving this final skill training session, we want to be sure you are aware of a simple fact: *No marriage mentor, no matter how competent, is equipped to handle every situation.* You need to recognize that sooner or later, if you do enough marriage mentoring, an issue will arise that requires professional help. We devote an appendix to this topic in *The Complete Guide to Marriage Mentoring.* But, in case you have not read that book, we want to provide you with an exercise that will expose you to the fundamentals.

When to Take Action (8 MINUTES)

You are on the front lines. As marriage mentors, you are likely to be among the first people to know when and if a couple needs serious help that goes beyond marriage mentoring (in the case of major depression, for example). In spite of the continuing stigma of psychological treatment and the belief that families — especially in evangelical circles — should be able to solve their personal problems without outside help, mental health professionals can be of great value in helping hurting couples find the healing comfort of the Holy Spirit.

Following is a list of questions to help you determine whether a mentoree is dealing with an issue that needs professional intervention. If you answer yes to any of these "red flag" issues, it's time to refer. Since you are probably not already mentoring a couple, the point of this exercise is to simply be aware of the questions to consider if you ever suspect one of your mentorees needs help. Read through the list with your spouse and briefly strategize how you might proceed if one of your mentorees displayed any of these "symptoms":

- Is one of your mentorees painfully silent for long periods and withdrawn socially (even with his or her spouse)?
- Is one of your mentorees quitting a job for no rational reason or making other sudden unexplainable decisions?
- Is one of your mentorees obsessed with exercise and diet to the point that you think she (rarely does this occur in males) might have an eating disorder?
- Is one of your mentorees practicing any form of self-mutilation in the form of cuts or burns?
- Is one of your mentorees showing an excessive fear of a particular family member, other relative, or family friend?

- Does one of your mentorees have long periods of feeling worthless, helpless, guilty, or lethargic? Does he or she suffer from depression?
- Does one of your mentorees blow up with anger? Is he or she a threat to someone's physical well-being, especially the fiancée or spouse and children?
- Does one of your mentorees report hearing voices that others do not hear? Does he or she hallucinate or is he or she out of touch with reality?
- Is one of your mentorees having serious problems with sleep, such as insomnia, repeated wakefulness at night, frequent nightmares, or sleeping too much?
- Does one of your mentorees have morbid thoughts, talk about death a lot? Is he or she suicidal?
- Does one of your mentorees drive while drinking? Do you suspect a problem with excessive drinking or drug use?
- Does one of your mentorees experience relatively brief periods of intense anxiety? Does he or she suffer from panic attacks?

Of course, this is not an exhaustive list of every possible issue that may require professional help, but it covers the most common ones.

THE NEXT STEPS

Corresponds to the Appendixes for Marriage Mentors section
of *The Complete Guide to Marriage Mentoring.*

CHOOSING YOUR PERSONAL MARRIAGE MENTOR TRACK

You are on the brink of concluding your training sessions to become a marriage mentor. You've covered:

- The Preliminaries
- The Big Picture
- Marriage Mentoring as a Man
- The Essential Training Skills

Now view this brief video that recaps or overviews a few more important pieces of information to help you round out your experience.

Play the DVD segment for session 10. (4 MINUTES)
Use the following space to take notes if you wish.

In session 2, you completed an exercise that we are going to have you complete once more. Only this time you are doing so with more knowledge and self-exploration under your belt.

Which Track Do You Lean Into? (5 MINUTES)

Where are you best gifted to be marriage mentors? As you did in session 2, place a number in the corner of the marriage mentoring triangle below that best represents your percentage of desire to mentor each type of couple (the three numbers should total 100). Only this time, you are determining this percentage together with your spouse, not as an individual.

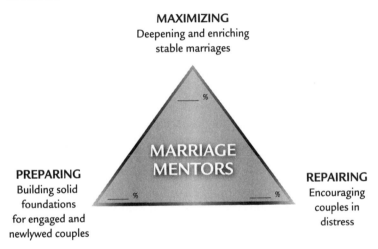

MAXIMIZING
Deepening and enriching
stable marriages

_____ %

MARRIAGE MENTORS

PREPARING
Building solid
foundations
for engaged and
newlywed couples

_____ %

REPAIRING
Encouraging
couples in
distress

_____ %

After you have completed this portion of the exercise, you may want to revisit the exercise in session 2 (page 25) to see if and how your leanings may have changed or been influenced by each other. By the way, if one of the three marriage tracks still does not seem to be a clear "winner," that's okay. This is merely a tool for helping you to determine where your particular passion for mentoring might be.

DEVELOPING YOUR OWN MARRIAGE MENTORING STYLE

In session 9, you explored "Being Yourself and Going with the Flow." Because that skill has a lot to do with developing your own style as a marriage mentor couple, we won't spend much additional time on it here. But we do want to highlight the idea of bringing your personal uniqueness as a couple into the mentoring relationship.

With more and more experience you will begin to log creative ideas that work especially well for you. This may be something as simple and tangential as making milkshakes whenever you have a mentoring meeting (a kind of "signature" on your mentoring sessions) or something more meaningful, such as having routine prayer time with your mentorees.

Getting Creative (8 MINUTES)

This exercise is designed to get you thinking about what your combined personalities will do for a mentoring relationship. Complete these sentence-stems together as a couple:

Because of our unique personalities, our marriage mentoring sessions are sure to include ...

_____

_____

Because of our unique personalities, our marriage mentoring sessions are sure to probably never include ...

_____

_____

Because of our unique personalities, our marriage mentorees are likely to ...

_____

_____

Because of our unique personalities, our marriage mentorees are not likely to ...

_____

_____

When it comes to being creative and developing your own style, by the way, you may want to explore our book *51 Creative Ideas for Marriage Mentors*. It is chock-full of innovative ways to make your marriage mentoring connections fun, meaningful, and memorable.

LEADING A SMALL GROUP AS A MARRIAGE MENTOR

One of the most helpful ways to augment and extend the influence you will have as marriage mentors is to help get your mentorees plugged into a small group experience. If you and your spouse have ever participated in a small group with other couples, you know firsthand how valuable such a community can be.

Whether you are mentoring couples who are preparing for lifelong love, repairing a love gone bad, or moving a relationship from good to great, small groups are an invaluable asset to most marriages.

In session 2 of this training manual, you briefly explored the structure of a typical marriage mentoring ministry. You may want to revisit the diagram right now (page 27) to see how it can all filter down to small group ministry.

Your Small Group Experience (10 MINUTES)

Review with your spouse any small groups you are currently participating in as a couple, or have participated in in the past.

- What small groups have you been in together?
- What did or do your small groups do for your marriage?
- What are the benefits of being in a couples small group (versus a same-sex small group)?
- What might be the benefits of actually participating in a small group with your mentoree couple?

Of course, your pastoral staff/church may already have a couples small group ministry to plug into. If not, explore the possibility of getting one up and running. It doesn't take much. Just a few other couples to gather at an appointed time—whether it's once a week for six weeks (the most common format) or something else.

RECRUITING OTHER MARRIAGE MENTORS

Another important step to consider at this juncture is how you might help to continue waking up the sleeping giant in the church by recruiting other potential marriage mentors. You may recall what we said in the introduction to this training manual: "There are close to 400,000 churches in America. If just one-third of these churches would recruit and train ten mentor couples each, that would mean one million marriage mentors."

We'd love to see you become involved in helping others in your community become marriage mentors. Here's a very brief exercise to help you personalize this.

Who Else Can Mentor Couples? (3 MINUTES)

Chances are that you can think of another couple who would make good marriage mentors. Talk with your partner about who that might be. Why do you think the couple you have in mind would do this well? When would it be appropriate to recruit them?

If you find it helpful, you may even want to use one of the marriage mentor recruiting segments on the DVD (both a five-minute and a two-minute version are included). The DVD also includes a four-minute video clip targeted directly to potential mentorees.

> NOTE: If you're doing this training as an individual couple, you may want to view these promos now if you haven't done so previously.

WHAT YOU WILL FIND FOR MARRIAGE MENTORS AT WWW.REALRELATIONSHIPS.COM

Believing that the sustainability of your marriage mentoring ministry requires more than just a book and DVD kit, we want to continually resource you with materials and contacts that will prove helpful as you get up and running. For this purpose we have developed a website just for you: www.RealRelationships.com.

There you will find downloadable forms, assessment tools, mentoring tips, articles featuring the latest information and research, a question forum, conference and seminar announcements, a resource library, and a network to connect with other marriage mentors. Don't miss out on all the latest updates — we want to be there for you! And please get in touch to tell us your stories, successes, and challenges. We love hearing from you.

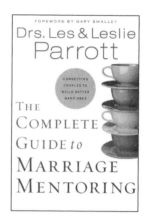
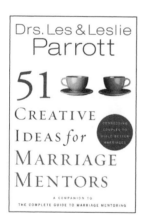

Marriage Mentor Training Manual for Husbands/Wives

You've spent years learning how to make your marriage work. Now it's time to share your knowledge and experience. Designed to be used with the *Marriage Mentor Training and Recruiting* DVD, these ten-session manuals equip the two of you to help a less experienced couple arrive at the stability, comfort, and richness you've achieved in your own relationship.

Husbands Manual, Softcover: 0-310-27165-7
Wives Manual, Softcover: 0-310-27125-8

Complete Resource Kit for Marriage Mentoring

Contains ten-session DVD, featuring the Parrotts as well as actual marriage mentors and mentorees, and nearly 100 minutes of video instruction that coincides with the husbands and wives training manuals. Works equally well for couples training on their own or in a group setting (leader's guide included). Also included in the kit: one copy each of *The Complete Guide to Marriage Mentoring, 51 Creative Ideas for Marriage Mentors, Husbands Training Manual,* and *Wives Training Manual.*

Boxed kit: 0-310-27110-X

Love Talk Starters
275 Questions to Get Your Conversations Going

Drs. Les & Leslie Parrott

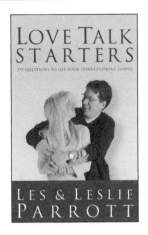

In this companion book, *Love Talk Starters*, you will find engaging, intriguing, and revealing conversation starters. Some questions are just for fun, some will educate you about your spouse's life, and still others will drill down on some more serious topics. Use these simple conversation starters and begin communicating your way into a happier, healthier, and stronger relationship today.

Softcover: 0-310-81047-7

Just the Two of Us
Love Talk Meditations for Couples

Drs. Les & Leslie Parrott

Les and Leslie Parrott share communication insights and wisdom for couples that are newly married or have been married for forty years. The Parrotts write in a very compelling and transparent way using their personal experiences with communication challenges in their own marriage. A wonderful companion to *Love Talk*. Some of the titles of the meditations include: What Were You Thinking?, You're Reading My Mind, and The Talks That Tie Us Together.

Gift book: 0-310-80381-0

Interested in hosting the Parrotts for one of their highly acclaimed seminars? It's easy. Just visit www.RealRelationships.com to learn more and complete a speaking request form.

Les and Leslie speak to thousands in dozens of cities annually. They are entertaining, thought-provoking, and immeasurably practical. One minute you'll be laughing and the next you'll sit still in silence as they open your eyes to how you can make your relationship all it's meant to be.

"I've personally benefited from the Parrotts' seminar. You can't afford to miss it."

GARY SMALLEY

"Les and Leslie's seminars can make the difference between you having winning relationships and disagreeable ones."

ZIG ZIGLAR

"The Parrotts will revolutionize your relationships."

JOSH MCDOWELL

"Without a doubt, Les and Leslie are the best at what they do and they will help you become a success where it counts most."

JOHN C. MAXWELL

Learn more about the Parrotts' "Becoming
Soul Mates Seminar" and their new "Love Talk Seminar."

*Click on www.RealRelationships.com
to bring them to your community.*

We want to hear from you. Please send your comments about this book to us in care of zreview@zondervan.com. Thank you.

GRAND RAPIDS, MICHIGAN 49530 USA

ZONDERVAN.COM/
AUTHORTRACKER